Little Moo's
BIG
Adventure

Little Moo's BIG Adventure

Mona K. McVay

iUniverse®

LITTLE MOO'S BIG ADVENTURE

Scripture taken from the New King James Version. Copyright © 1979, 1980, 1982 by Thomas Nelson, Inc. Used by permission. All rights reserved.

This is a work of fiction. All the characters, names, incidents, organizations, and dialogue in this novel are either the products of the author's imagination or are used fictitiously.

iUniverse books may be ordered through booksellers or by contacting:

iUniverse
1663 Liberty Drive
Bloomington, IN 47403
www.iuniverse.com
1-800-Authors (1-800-288-4677)

Because of the dynamic nature of the internet, any web addresses or links contained in this book may have changed since publication and may no longer be valid. The views expressed in this work are solely those of the author and do not necessarily reflect the views of the publisher, and the publisher hereby disclaims any responsibility for them.

Any people depicted in stock imagery provided by Getty Images are models, and such images are being used for illustrative purposes only. Certain stock imagery © Getty Images.

ISBN: 978-1-5320-3997-3 (sc)
ISBN: 978-1-5320-3996-6 (e)

Library of Congress Control Number: 2018907406

Print information available on the last page.

iUniverse rev. date: 07/28/2018

Little Moo's Big Adventure

"Mommy, why can't I play with those cows across the street?"

"Well, honey, we can't get over there because we are fenced in."

"I sure would like to play in that big field, Mommy. Can we jump the fence and go over there?"

"No, darling. There are too many cars that go way too fast on this country road. I wouldn't want my Little Moo to get hurt. We belong here to graze, as Grandma taught us to. Besides, I would miss you if you were to go over there."

Little Moo wandered off, pouting. He kept hearing the other calves playing and began to think of a way to get out of the fence.

Maybe I could crawl underneath the fence, he thought as he went to take a dip in the pond. Moo kept pondering his adventure.

When Mom falls asleep tonight, I will sneak out and try crawling underneath the fence.

Nighttime came, and Little Moo sneaked out. He headed toward the fence, bent down, and attempted to crawl under it, but he found out he was too big to fit through the fence.

Hmm, I wonder if I could jump over the fence.

With all his might, Little Moo backed up and took a running leap, but he failed. As he backed up again, he heard a big, loud semitruck coming down the road, but he ran and leaped again.

His curious little mind kept churning up ideas as he backed up once again and took a running leap—but to no avail. He got his front left hoof stuck in the fence and fell backward, startled by the howling coyotes. As he struggled to get loose, it only tightened the grip on his hoof. The howls were getting closer, and he was getting scared and started to cry but was determined to get loose.

Little Moo started praying. *Dear God, please, please, please* help me now! As Little Moo gave his leg one hard kick, his foot became free and he ran like lightning until he was safe back beside his mom in the barn.

The next morning, Little Moo felt a bit tired from being up later than his normal bedtime, so he slept in until his mom came and woke him.

"Little Moo, you better get up now. It's breakfast time."

He stretched and yawned.

"Okay, Mom. I'll be out there in a minute."

As she walked out of the barn and went to eat her breakfast, Little Moo turned over and fell back asleep.

His mom came back in and woke him up again.

"Honey, aren't you feeling well?"

She felt his nose to see if it was warm, but it was wet and cold.

"Yes, Mommy, I feel fine."

"Okay, just checking. You better get up now."

So Little Moo got up like his mother told him to.

After he ate his breakfast, he saw Mr. Horse over by the fence, and he went over to talk to him.

"Mr. Horse, you're pretty smart. If you wanted to leave your pasture, how would you go about doing it?"

"Well, in the first place, I wouldn't want to. Why do you want to leave your pasture, Little Moo?" Mr. Horse asked him.

"There is nobody to play with over here, and see all those cows over there across the street? It'd be so much fun over there."

"The grass may not always be greener on the other side of the fence, my little friend," Mr. Horse told him.

"What's that supposed to mean, Mr. Horse?"

"You will understand one day, Little Moo. You will understand."

So Little Moo went wandering off to ponder what Mr. Horse had said.

Hmm, the grass may not always be greener on the other side. I will go ask Mrs. Goose what that means.

So Little Moo went to find Mrs. Goose pecking the ground by the chicken coop.

"Hi, Mrs. Goose. I wonder if you could answer a question for me," Little Moo said.

"Good morning, Little Moo. I will try. What might be your question?"

"Well, I guess I have two questions really. I was wondering, If you wanted to leave this pasture, how would you go about doing so?"

As she was honking and laughing so hard, she said, "Oh, Little Moo, God gave me these wings. I could fly away if I wanted to, but I love it here. All the animals, you see, are fed by these nice people. God provides for us very well here, you silly calf. Now what was the other question?"

"What does 'The grass isn't always greener on the other side' mean?" Little Moo asked.

"Oh, you've been talking to Mr. Horse, haven't you?"

"Yes, how did you know, Mrs. Goose?"

"I've heard him say that many a time. It means something may appear to look better than it actually is. Why would you want to leave this pasture anyway?"

"I have no one my age to play with. And see over there across the street? They all seem so happy, and it looks like a lot of fun."

"Well, Little Moo, just be happy over here, sweetie. If you left, everyone would miss you."

Little Moo hung his head and walked off to think about what Mrs. Goose had said. He went to the big oak tree and lay down, looking across the street, still wishing he could somehow just go check it out.

As he drifted off to sleep, he happened to remember the kids who lived there sometimes left the gate open when they stopped by to visit them.

I could sneak out when they get home, Little Moo thought.

When Little Moo woke from his nap, he looked up at the sky and saw dark clouds forming, which gave him another idea. *Looks like rain,* he thought.

He heard the school bus approaching and ran to the gated fence, but the kids ran up to the house without stopping to say hi.

Well, they must be in a hurry for some reason. I will have to try my other idea tonight after Mom falls asleep.

The rain started falling as his mom went into the barn for the evening. Little Moo waited for his mom to fall asleep before he tiptoed out. He went over to the fence and started digging a hole big enough to crawl underneath so he could get to the other side. He was getting wet from the rain, but the ground softened enough from the rain so he could dig easily.

He heard Mr. Owl above him on the phone lines.

"Little Moo, I heard you want to escape over to the other side. You know, once you get over there, how do you plan on getting into that fence?"

"I will just have to dig another hole," Little Moo told him.

"You are a foolish little fella. Don't you know what happens to those cows after they get a certain weight?"

"No, what happens to them, Mr. Owl?" Little Moo asked.

"Well, the way you're digging you will find out soon enough. Mr. Horse told you correctly. The grass may only appear to be greener on the other side, but you will find out the real meaning once you get over there."

"It can't be all that bad. They all look and sound so happy all of the time."

"You will find out soon enough. And what happens after that—well, I just hope it won't be too late."

"Oh, Mr. Owl, you are just trying to scare me. I'm sure I will be just fine, making new friends running and playing."

"Oh, you will be running all right! Hoo, hoo, hoo." Mr. Owl flew away laughing.

Little Moo didn't pay any attention to Mr. Owl and kept on digging. After a little while, he crawled out from underneath the fence, looked both ways, up and down the road, before crossing, and made it to the other side safely. Then Little Moo began to dig another hole to get to his final destination. He dug faster and faster as the rain kept falling down harder and harder.

After another hour went by, he finally made it. He was where he wanted to be. Little Moo was so excited that he leaped for joy.

However, what he didn't know was that word got out about him wanting to go play with those other cows, and everyone in his pasture got together and had a plan in case he accomplished getting to the other side.

Little Moo fell fast asleep underneath a big tree by the water hole. When he woke up the next morning, all those other cows were looking at him. Little Moo heard them whispering. Getting up, he spotted a cute girl cow with red earrings in her ears and two red bows. She was looking at him too.

"Hello, everyone, my name is Little Moo. I live across the road where that big house is and the big red barn. You all always look like you have a lot of fun over here, and I don't have anyone to play with over there, just my mom, and she gets tired too fast. What's everyone's name?" Little Moo asked.

"My name is Bull, and this here is Bruno. We are brothers, and we kind of run this place."

The cute, tan girl cow came walking up to Little Moo and introduced herself.

"My name is Melissa, but my family and friends call me Missy for short. What is your name?"

"Hi, my name is Little Moo. My family and friends call me Little Moo."

Missy started laughing. "You're cute and funny."

Little Moo started blushing.

"All right, all right, run along now, Missy. I need to tell Moo some things."

"It was nice meeting you, Missy."

"Bye, Little Moo. See you later."

She walked off and went to the pond, looked back at him, tripped on a stick, and fell into the water.

Little Moo laughed as he watched her and winked at her.

"Okay, okay, listen up, Little Moo. You can't stay here in this field unless you want to go to the meat market and end up as a T-bone steak."

"Bull, Bull, don't just blurt it out like that! Good Lord, brother! Don't you have any common sense?"

"No! I think that's what happened to my daddy! No, no, I don't want to end up like my daddy." Little Moo started to cry.

"Little Moo," Bruno said, "calm down, little buddy. You are not going to the meat market. Do you want to stay over here, or do you want to go back home?"

"I don't want to go to the meat market!" Little Moo was still sobbing.

Missy heard Little Moo shouting and crying and wanted so bad to come over to him. But Bull gave her a look that said, "Stay back," so she did.

Bull added, "If you don't want to go to the meat market, then I suggest you go back to your home. Your mom is probably worried about you."

"Moo, I will help you go back home. Come with me," said Bruno.

"But I want to stay and play with Missy and meet the others. How long can I stay before it's too late?" Little Moo asked.

"You have plenty of time, Little Moo. Let's go tell your mom you are over here so she will stop worrying about you."

Little Moo followed Bruno to the fence.

"So, how did you get over here in the first place?" Bruno asked.

"I dug underneath the fence at home and crawled underneath. Then I walked over here and did the same thing. It was storming big-time too. That's how I was able to get over here," Little Moo said excitedly.

"Oh, I see. Is that where you dug underneath the fence?" Bruno asked.

Bruno saw his owner filling in the hole with cement as they were walking to the fence.

"Yeah, yeah it is. What's he doing? Who is he? Is he the one who took my daddy to the market?"

"Yes, I'm afraid he is. Never mind, because that's not going to happen to you. Is that your mommy over there? She looks just like you."

"Yeah, it is. Hey, Mom! Mom! It's me, Little Moo. I'm okay!"

Maggie looked up when she heard her son calling after her.

"Little Moo! There you are! I have been so anxious about you, not knowing where you have been! How in the world did you get over there? I've been worried sick about you! Will you please get back home now, son? Mommy has been missing you something terrible!"

"What's your mommy's name, Little Moo?"

"Maggie. Her name is Maggie."

"Maggie, my name is Bruno. My twin brother and I run this pasture. Little Moo is just fine. He wants to stay and play a little while. I told him we needed to let you know where he was first, and then I would see to it that he came back home safely where he belonged."

Bruno was watching Little Moo watching Missy, looking back at her, and then Bruno looked back at Maggie.

"I do believe he has a crush on one of our little heifers."

Maggie was watching her son too. "Yes, I do believe so too. Little Moo, if you promise me that you will come home before it starts getting dark, you can play, as long as you stay out of trouble. You mind Bruno and his brother, okay?"

"I will, Mommy! I promise. I love you! Thank you so very much! See you after while!" And he went running to the pond where Missy was.

"You have quite the son there, Maggie."

"Yes, yes I do. Thank you. Bruno, I've heard some awful things about your pasture. Is it really true that some bulls and cows get sent off?"

"Yes, I am afraid it is true."

"Bruno! Come on! We have work to do!" Bull was hollering at his brother because he didn't want Bruno to say any more about their pasture business.

"It's been a pleasure talking to you, Maggie, but I have to run now. I will be sure to have Little Moo back in time for supper."

"Okay, Bruno. Nice meeting you, and thank you."

"Nice meeting you too, Maggie. We shall talk again soon, when Bull is busy. You're very pretty."

Bruno walked back to where Bull was, looked back at Maggie, and winked at her.

In the meantime, Little Moo and Missy played in the pond, laughing and splashing, having a fun time.

"So how old are you, Little Moo?" Missy asked him.

"I'm three months old. How old are you?" Little Moo answered her.

"I'm two months old. So you don't have any brothers or sisters?" Missy asked.

"Nope, it's just me. Do you have any brothers or sisters?" he asked Missy.

"I have an older brother who is three years old and a sister who is two years old, and they are over there." Missy pointed over to where they were.

"What are their names?" Little Moo asked.

"Their names are Mindy and Michael. So why did you want to come over here, Little Moo?"

"I spotted you right off and just knew it would be worth coming over to check you out. I was right. You were worth coming over here."

Missy flashed her baby brown eyes at him and fluttered her eyelashes. They laughed and played all day long, as Missy showed him around the pasture and introduced him to everyone there.

Bruno came looking for him as the ranch hand started feeding them. Missy let Little Moo eat some of her food. They took turns. Little Moo didn't want to go home and leave Missy.

"Okay, Little Moo. It's time to go, buddy. We promised your mom you would go back before it got dark. Tell Missy and everyone bye."

"It was very nice to meet you all. I've had lots of fun, and I hope I can visit again real soon," Little Moo said.

"I don't want you to leave, Little Moo," Missy said as she started to cry.

"I don't want to leave you either, Missy. Don't worry. I will find a way for us to be together again. I promise. Don't cry, baby doll."

Little Moo rubbed up against her nose and wiped her tears away with his head.

Bruno and Little Moo started walking toward the fence, and Missy started following them.

"Bruno, do you think I could come back and play some more tomorrow?"

"I don't know, son. How would you get back over here?"

"Well, I have some more ideas. How are we going to get back over right now?" Little Moo asked anxiously.

"We leave the gate open down here all the time, but you see these steel bars? You have to be really careful so you don't step through them."

"Hmm, you could jump over them, couldn't you?"

"If you think you can, but I wouldn't," Bruno advised.

They reached the gate and stopped. Missy was a little way back, watching and listening to their every move.

"Okay, watch me, Little Moo, and step where I step."

"Okay, Bruno. I will."

So that's what he did. Little Moo followed Bruno's every move, and they both made it across the bars safely to the other side. Missy still watched closely in the distance.

They looked both ways, up and down the road, before they walked across the street to Little Moo's gate—and it was open. *The kids must have forgotten to latch it again,* Little Moo thought.

"Okay, Little Moo, you are home safely again. Go let your mom know you're back, and then you best eat your supper."

"Okay, Bruno. I will. Thanks."

After Little Moo found his mom, she was so happy he was back where he belonged and rubbed his nose with hers. Little Moo then ate his supper and went into the barn to lie down, and he fell right to sleep. He was plumb tuckered out after playing all day with Missy.

The next morning, he got right up, ate his breakfast, and then went right over to the fence to see if he could find Missy. She was at the fence waiting for him, grazing on the grass.

"Good morning, sunshine! How are you, beautiful?" Little Moo asked her.

"Good morning, Little Moo! I'm okay. How are you?" Missy asked.

"I feel good. I slept like a log. Did you sleep well?" Little Moo asked.

"Yeah, I slept off and on. I kept thinking about you and if we would be together today or not."

"Don't worry your pretty little head, Missy. I believe we are meant to be together and God will see to it that everything will work out for us."

"Okay, Little Moo. I saw you leave across the bars last night. I could try and get over that way."

"That's a great idea. After my people go to work, they usually leave the gate open. You could try then. Oh, here he comes now, leaving for work. Wait a minute."

Mr. Davis drove off and left the gate open for Mrs. Davis, just as Little Moo knew he would.

She would be leaving shortly after him, within ten to fifteen minutes.

"Okay, Missy, go over to the bars and be really careful. Don't let your hoof slip through the bars."

"Okay, I will be careful."

She walked over, stepped on the bars very carefully, and made it across just fine. Then she looked up and down the street before she crossed the road and came through the gate.

"I made it, Little Moo! I did it!" She rubbed noses with him, pleased she had made it across safely.

"Okay, now we have to hide for a little bit until we can come up with an idea to keep you over here."

"Okay. That sounds good."

When Mrs. Davis left, Little Moo and Missy came out of hiding and went to the pond over behind the other big barn that was blue, which was out of sight of his mom.

"You have a nice big pasture too, Little Moo. I'd love to stay here forever with you."

"I'd love for you to, but wouldn't you miss your siblings and Bruno and Bull?"

"Well, I would miss Bruno, but Bull—he is mean. And as for my brothers and sisters, they just think I'm a baby, and I get in the way all the time."

"Oh, but they would miss you, wouldn't they? I missed you the moment I had to leave last night."

"Aw, that's so sweet, Little Moo. I missed you too. That's why I couldn't sleep very well."

Little Moo was telling her all about his farm and his friends as they played and grazed.

Mr. Owl flew by, landing on the feeding bin. "Well, hello there, Little Moo. Who is your little friend?"

"Hello, Hootie. This is Missy. Missy, this is Hootie, or Mr. Owl."

"Well, hello, Missy. Where did you come from, as if I didn't know?"

"Don't answer him, Missy. He knows already. Go away, Hootie. You try your best just to rain on my parade all the time."

"Well, excuse me, Little Moo. Carry on then." Hootie flew away.

"I'm sorry about him, Missy. He can be nice, but here lately he's been really mean."

"Maybe he just needs to find a girlfriend, like I did. Will you be my girlfriend, Missy?"

Missy flashed her big brown eyes at Little Moo and giggled. Mrs. Goose wandered over to them and started talking.

"How are you doing, Little Moo? This must be Missy. I've been watching you two all morning."

"How does everyone know my name?" Missy asked.

"Oh, dear, this is a small farm. Everyone knows everyone's business around here. No point in hiding."

"Mrs. Goose, we are trying to think of a way for Missy to stay here for good. Do you have any suggestions for how she could?"

"Well, well, Little Moo. It appears that all the cows over yonder are disappearing before our very eyes. We may not need an excuse. Take a look for yourselves."

They both looked across the farm and saw a truck loading up cows. They got out of the pond and started walking to the fence to see a lot better.

Little Moo looked back at Mrs. Goose. "Thanks, Mrs. Goose! Thanks a lot."

"You're welcome, Little Moo."

They got to the fence to see Bull and Bruno.

"Bruno! What's going on?" Little Moo yelled out to Bruno.

"Remember what I told you yesterday, buddy?"

"Yeah."

"Well, that is what is going on. Good thing Missy came over to you when she did."

"What is going to happen to you and Bull?"

"I believe Bull is staying here. I heard the human tell your human he could have his pick of me or Bull."

"Awesome! So when are you coming over?"

"I don't know for sure, but probably after they move all of the other cows."

"Well, finally some good news! Why do you think Bull is going to stay there, Bruno?"

"I overheard the humans say they are bringing over an older heifer who can't have babies anymore, to give Bull some company."

"I'm so glad. No one should be alone in life. Hey, maybe you and Mom can keep each other company too. Well, you know. Maybe you can be my other daddy."

Bruno started laughing and said, "I'd like that, son. I'd like that very much."

After all the cows had been moved to their final destination, Little Moo's human came home and walked over to see about getting Bruno. Just in time for supper too.

Mr. Davis walked Bruno over to their farm and led him to the fence. Maggie was eating away, not aware of him approaching her.

"Well, hello, Maggie girl. I brought you someone to befriend. This is Bruno. He is a real nice bull. I believe you two will get along pretty well."

Maggie looked up when Mr. Davis said Bruno. She looked at him and then Bruno, as if she didn't understand.

Bruno winked and nodded his head at her, as if to tell her he would explain. Before Mr. Davis left, he walked Bruno into the fenced farmyard, patted both Bruno and Maggie, and then went into his house.

Little Moo and Missy came around the corner to see Bruno and Maggie talking as they were eating their supper.

"Hello, Bruno. I am so happy you are a part of our family now. Mom, are you glad Bruno is here with us now?"

Maggie giggled and turned to her son. "Yes, Little Moo, I am very glad. And I am glad Missy is here with us too. You seem like a very nice girl, Missy."

"How did you know about Missy, Mom? I came over to introduce her to you."

"Oh, I've heard it through the grapevine, so to speak. You know Hootie can't keep his mouth shut about anything."

"That is true. I should have known. Speaking of Hootie, I haven't seen him since early this morning," Little Moo said.

After he said that, they heard something in the air. When they all looked up, they saw Hootie, a female owl, and three baby owls flying behind him.

"Aw, it looks like everyone is happy and has someone to keep them company now," Little Moo said as he looked around and saw Hootie and his family. Little Moo saw Mr. and Mrs. Goose in the pond, swimming around, and Mr. and Mrs. Horse by the big oak tree, eating leaves off the tree.

Moral of the Story

If ever you think something looks and sounds better than what you have right now, always remember to do the following:

Trust in the Lord with all your heart and lean not on your own understanding; but in all your ways, acknowledge Him and He shall direct your path. (Proverbs 3:5–6 New King James Version)

About the Author

Mona K. McVay was born in Wichita, Kansas, but she has lived most of her life in Oklahoma. Mona enjoys playing with her two shih tzus, Maggie and Melody, and Sadie, a teacup Yorkie. She truly believes if we put our trust in God in all things, He will see us through everything. Mona currently lives in Collinsville, Oklahoma.

www.ingramcontent.com/pod-product-compliance
Lightning Source LLC
Chambersburg PA
CBHW030544290526
45786CB00004B/1858